Welcome

Colette
Burke

Managing Director
Cadbury Ltd.

Welcome to Cadbury World at Bournville - the visitor centre devoted entirely to chocolate.

As a nation we have a passionate love of chocolate - as a food, a gift, a treat, a comfort, a snack or as a simple indulgence. And we have a fascination with chocolate, a desire to know more about where it comes from and how it is made.

I hope that your visit to Cadbury World is a very enjoyable one, and that together with this brochure we are able to give you a unique insight into our company, our history and our chocolate.

Cadbury
WORLD

Contents

Cadbury
WORLD

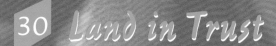

The First name in Chocolate

Cadbury's Dairy Milk is Britain's most popular chocolate taste.

John Cadbury started his one-man business in 1824.

Today, Cadbury spans the globe.

Brits love chocolate. Only the Swiss consume more per person per year.

The Cadbury Story

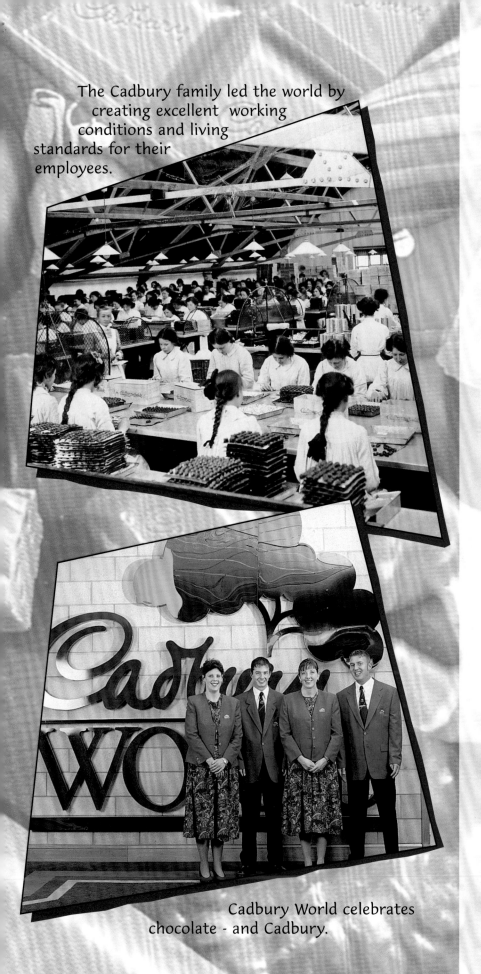

The Cadbury family led the world by creating excellent working conditions and living standards for their employees.

Cadbury World celebrates chocolate - and Cadbury.

Chocolate - one of life's little luxuries.

From its small beginnings, Cadbury today holds a leading position in the world of chocolate.

This astounding growth is founded on the success of Cadbury's Dairy Milk. From its launch in 1905, the unique recipe of 'CDM' has helped make it one of the world's famous brands.

But the Cadbury story is more than just the story of chocolate.

● It's the story of a family whose personal beliefs inspired the way they worked.

● It's the story of the creation of a community.

● It's the story of far-sighted developments in employee welfare.

● It's a story that reflects many social changes in Britain.

● And it's a story of fun and enjoyment.

Cadbury World - and this brochure - is dedicated to telling you that story.

Chocolate Know-how

3 The beans are laid on mats and dried in the sun, then packed into sacks for transport.

2 For about six days, the beans ferment under plantain or banana leaves, and the pulp drains away.

A rich brown coloured bean shows good quality. Purple or mouldy beans show they have not been fermented or dried properly

It takes a whole year's crop from one tree to make one pound of cocoa.

1 The cocoa pods are split open and the white beans in sticky pulp are scooped out.

The Raw Material

Cocoa trees grow in tropical areas near the equator. Ghana supplies most of our high quality cocoa.

The chocolate flavour develops as the beans are fermented and dried by the farmer. But it's only when they are roasted at our factory at Chirk in North Wales that you start to smell that wonderful chocolate aroma!

The liquid "mass" is also mixed with full cream milk and sugar and then dried to form "crumb".

Hot Chocolate, Drinking Chocolate

What's left after the cocoa butter is removed is called "press - cake". This can be ground into a fine powder to produce cocoa, which with the addition of sugar, becomes drinking chocolate. The cocoa butter is used later in the chocolate making process.

4 After roasting, the beans are 'kibbled' - broken into small pieces called nibs - and the shells removed - 'winnowed'.

5 At Chirk, the nibs are ground into a thick liquid - 'mass' - and about half the oily cocoa butter removed.

A selection of dried beans from a consignment is cut and assessed

Chocolate Know-how

We monitor the ingredients with instruments and computers and sometimes by sight.

Sweetened Condensed milk

↓

MIXED AND DRIED

↓

crumb

↓

PULVERISED

↓

MIXED AND REFINED

↓

CONCHED AND TEMPERED

Cocoa mass

Cocoa Butter

sugar

↓

MIXED AND REFINED

Cadbury's Bournville plain chocolate

Cadbury's DAIRY MILK

MIXED AND EVAPORATED

Full cream milk

sugar

Cocoa mass

Cocoa Butter

Cocoa Butter

Sweetened Condensed milk

MIXED AND REFINED

DRIED

Cadbury's CREAMY-WHITE **Buttons** CREAMY-WHITE CHOCOLATES

The recipe for Cadbury's chocolate is a secret known by only a few people.

Recipe for Success

Crumb - is the basis of all Cadbury's milk chocolate - is made in our Marlbrook plant near Hereford and transported to our factories at Bournville, and Somerdale near Bristol.

The addition of fresh milk makes the difference between plain and milk chocolate. White chocolate is made without the brown coloured cocoa mass.

We also add flavourings and a small amount of vegetable fat to chocolate, to get the texture and flavour just right.

Once the ingredients are mixed and refined they are pummelled back and forth for several hours. This *conching* develops the flavour and improves the smoothness.

Temper with Patience

Finally the chocolate is tempered - carefully mixed and cooled from about 50°C down to 29°C. Tempering produces chocolate with the famous Cadbury smoothness, gloss and 'snap'. It requires sophisticated machinery controlled by highly skilled workers.

Cadbury WORLD

Chocolate Know-how

Countlines

moulded

Cadbury's FRUIT & NUT — Milk Chocolate with Raisins & Almonds

Cadbury's WHOLE NUT — Milk Chocolate with Hazelnuts

Cadbury's DAIRY MILK — Milk Chocolate

Decker NOW MORE Chocolate!

The widest range of bars - sold by number rather than weight.

The simplest way to make a bar is to pour liquid chocolate - sometimes with added ingredients - into a mould.

The Creme Eggs sold each season placed one on top of the other, would be more than 1000 times higher than Mount Everest.

The Hazel Whirl i Roses' most popular choice.

selflines

One for the playground, one for the dinner party, but both from the same category - identical sweets packed in bags or boxes.

SEASONAL

Only available at special times of the year - so all the more desirable.

Roses, like Milk Tray, is an Assortment - the natural choice for gifts and special occasions.

Boxes, Bags & Bars

Cadbury's chocolate, delicious on its own, is also the key ingredient for a huge range of products; something for everybody, and every occasion.

Breaking the Mould

Although Cadbury's Dairy Milk is much the same now as when it was first produced, there's been fantastic innovation in how it's presented - from tiny miniatures, through chunky foil-wrapped Pocket Packs to staggering 1.25kg giant bars.

Counting on Cadbury

Bournville is home to our Moulded products and Assortments. Countlines - individually wrapped chocolate covered bars - are produced in Cadbury factories in Dublin, and Somerdale near Bristol.

An Annual Eggsplosion

The unique Cadbury Creme Egg far outsells any other. We only supply them from January to Easter, but many shops over-order to extend the selling season. Who can blame them?

Birth of a Bar

Our food technologists combined people's favourite ingredients in many different ways.

Customers in small "focus groups" told us they wanted a satisfying and convenient chocolate snack.

Many of today's best sellers are the result of Cadbury inspiration.

14

Within three months of its launch, 40 per cent of the UK population said they had tried Fuse.

New Product Development

Cadbury has always been an innovator in chocolate. Until 1915, chocolate assortments, packed in plush boxes, were simply too expensive for ordinary people. Then Cadbury produced an everyday selection, in a stylish but simple pack. Milk Tray became the best-selling boxed chocolate assortment ever.

Driving Innovation

Sometimes technology can be the spur - for example Flake, with its unique shape and texture. Sometimes an existing product is developed further - adding caramel to the already popular Wispa to produce Wispa Gold.

Launch of the Decade

And sometimes it's in response to changing lifestyle patterns - the incredibly successful Fuse was launched in 1996 after five years of development. It combines raisins, peanuts, cereal, fudge - and chocolate - into the ideal snack for busy young adults.

We tested many different recipes, names and wrappers, to get the perfect combination.

Forty million bars were delivered in the first week.

Four weeks after its launch, Cadbury's Fuse became the UK's best selling bar.

We market-tested a chocolate bar called Rondo. It became Wispa!

Cadbury WORLD

15

Halls of Montezuma

The Mayas included valuable cocoa beans in their "tribute" - taxes paid to their fearsome neighbours, the Aztecs.

As far back as AD 600 the Central American Maya people used cocoa to make a spicy drink called *chocolatl*.

The Aztec Emperor Montezuma lost his life and his empire to the Spaniard Don Hernan Cortes in AD 1520.

The Mayas would exchange ten cocoa beans for a rabbit - and a hundred for a slave!

The interpreter Malinche - baptised Donna Marina - told Don Cortes of the fabulous wealth in the Aztec city of Tenochtitlan.

After Montezuma's death, Cortes was made Captain General and Governor of Mexico. He rebuilt Tenochtitlan as Mexico City.

For two centuries the Aztec people controlled a mighty empire in what is now Mexico.

Chocolate's American Roots

The Aztecs couldn't grow cocoa trees because of their dry climate. Maya merchants brought cocoa from the Yucatan peninsula (in Mexico) by canoe and on foot.

The Aztec Emperor Montezuma was said to drink chocolate from golden goblets, served with great reverence, before visiting his wives.

Cortes - conqueror of the Aztecs

Astounded by his horses and cannons, the Aztecs thought Cortes was the legendary creator god Quetzalcoatl returning home.

Cortez captured Montezuma and through him tried to control his empire. But Aztec civilisation ended after a bloody struggle and a 75 day siege of Tenochtitlan.

Cortez returned to Spain in 1528, bringing cocoa beans and chocolate making equipment to Europe for the first time.

Cadbury WORLD

A Royal Secret

"Waked in the morning with my head in a sad taking through last night's drink. So rose and went out with Mr Creede to drink our morning draft, which he did give me chocolate to settle my stomach."

3 Samuel Pepys' diary, after the coronation of Charles II, April 1661.

1 Chocolate spread to France in 1615 when Anne, the daughter of King Philip II of Spain, married King Louis XIII. Her maid La Molina, brought the secret recipe with her.

2 The drink became fashionable at the opulent French Court.

In Britain, chocolate was known only as a drink for over 200 years.

Because cocoa beans were scarce and expensive, at first only the rich could enjoy chocolate.

Chocolate in Europe

Although the Spanish court tried to keep chocolate a secret, Catholic missionaries to America brought back recipes to France and Italy.

Chocolate was first advertised in Britain in 1657. Italian immigrant Francis White opened White's Chocolate House in 1693, in London's fashionable St James' Street. As well as various chocolate drinks, he sold ale, beer, coffee and snacks.

Growing Demand

In 1684, France captured Cuba and Haiti and set up cocoa plantations there. Chocolate became cheaper and more available as cocoa cultivation began to expand worldwide.

The Right Chemistry

Many of the early manufacturers of cocoa were apothecaries (chemists). They had the skills and equipment to heat, measure and blend the ingredients. And they believed the drink had medicinal properties.

4. In the 18th century, coffee and chocolate houses became widespread.

Not realising their value, English sailors threw cocoa beans overboard from captured Spanish ships,

Cadbury WORLD

Victorian Years

In 1831, John Cadbury rented a warehouse in Crooked Lane, near his shop.

Cocoa and chocolate were only a small part of the business until the 1870s.

Richard Tapper Cadbury, a draper, moved to Birmingham in 1794.

John Cadbury set up shop in 1824, next to his father's drapery business in Bull Street, Birmingham.

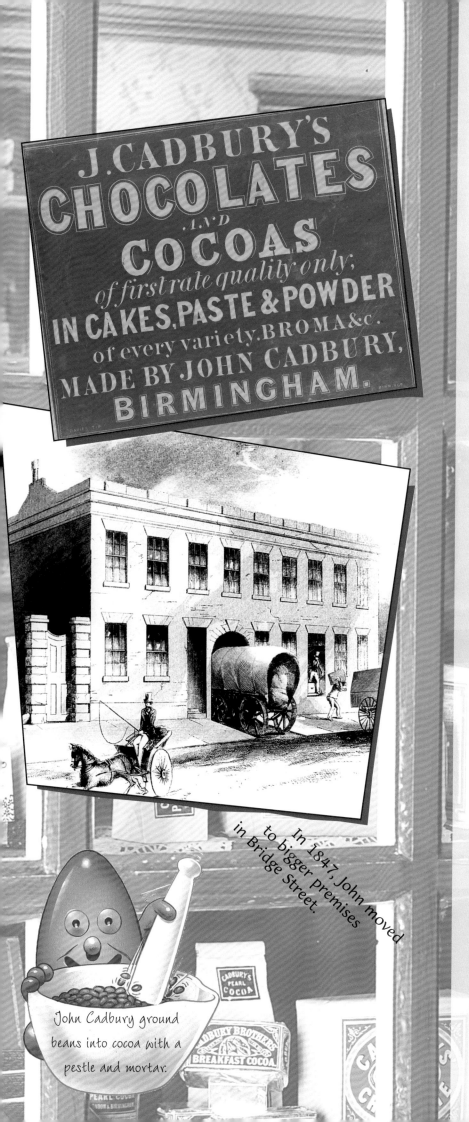

In 1847, John moved to bigger premises in Bridge Street.

John Cadbury ground beans into cocoa with a pestle and mortar.

Cadbury's first steps with chocolate

The Cadbury family were members of the Society of Friends - "Quakers". As nonconformists, Quakers were barred from the universities, so they couldn't enter professions like law or medicine. And because they were pacifists they wouldn't join the army or navy. As a result, many Quakers - like the Cadburys - went into commerce.

Quaker principles guided the Cadburys in business and social life. John Cadbury became a member of the growing Temperance movement.

Family Firm

When John rented the Bridge Street factory, his brother Benjamin left their father's drapery shop and joined him to form Cadbury Brothers.

We are Amused

In 1854, Cadbury Brothers gained the Royal Warrant, and could use the words "By Royal Appointment Manufacturers to the Queen".

Cadbury WORLD

21

Victorian Years

Drink **CADBURY'S** COCOA

ABSOLUTELY PURE and SOLUBLE

The brothers promoted their new product heavily.

"ABSOLUTELY PURE—THEREFORE BEST"

CADBURY'S C COCOA ESSENCE REGISTERED

With less cocoa butter, Cadbury's Cocoa Essence needed no additives.

With the Van Houten press, they were able to squeeze far more cocoa butter out of the beans.

Some manufacturers added brick dust or iron oxide to make their cocoa go further – ugh!

22

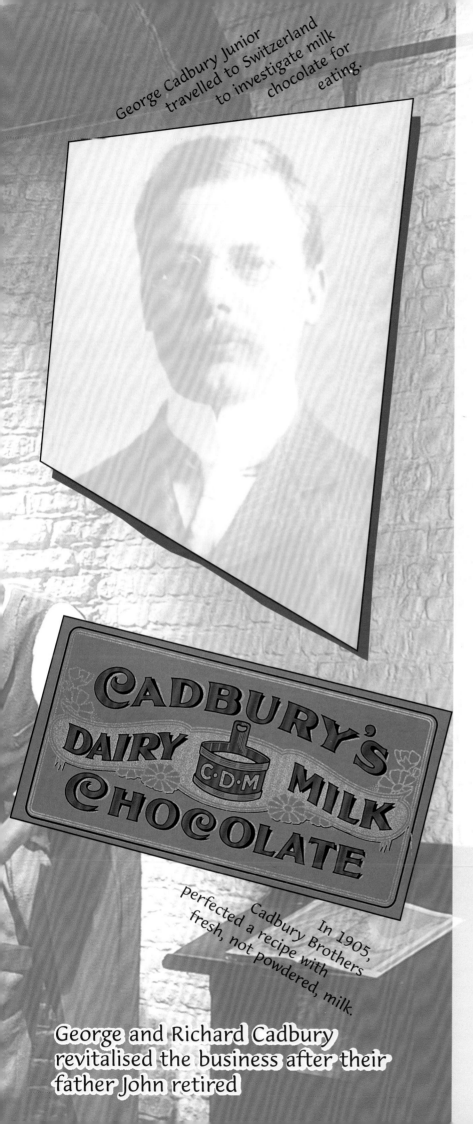

George Cadbury Junior travelled to Switzerland to investigate milk chocolate for eating.

Most Victorian cocoas were adulterated with potato starch or sago flour to soak up excess fat. But with the Dutch *Van Houten* cocoa press, George and Richard Cadbury were able to remove so much cocoa butter that no additives were necessary.

They submitted their new product for tests by doctors and chemists and advertised it as "Absolutely Pure, Therefore Best".

Chocolate for Eating

Chocolate was still a drink, although people may have occasionally nibbled on the solid blocks that were dissolved in water to make it. But in 1875 a Swiss milk chocolate bar actually designed for eating became a great success in Britain.

Cadbury Brothers launched their own milk chocolate in 1898, but it took seven years of research and effort before they perfected the recipe that became Cadbury's Dairy Milk.

CADBURY'S DAIRY MILK CHOCOLATE
C·D·M

In 1905, Cadbury Brothers perfected a recipe with fresh, not powdered, milk.

George and Richard Cadbury revitalised the business after their father John retired

Cadbury WORLD

23

Factory in a garden

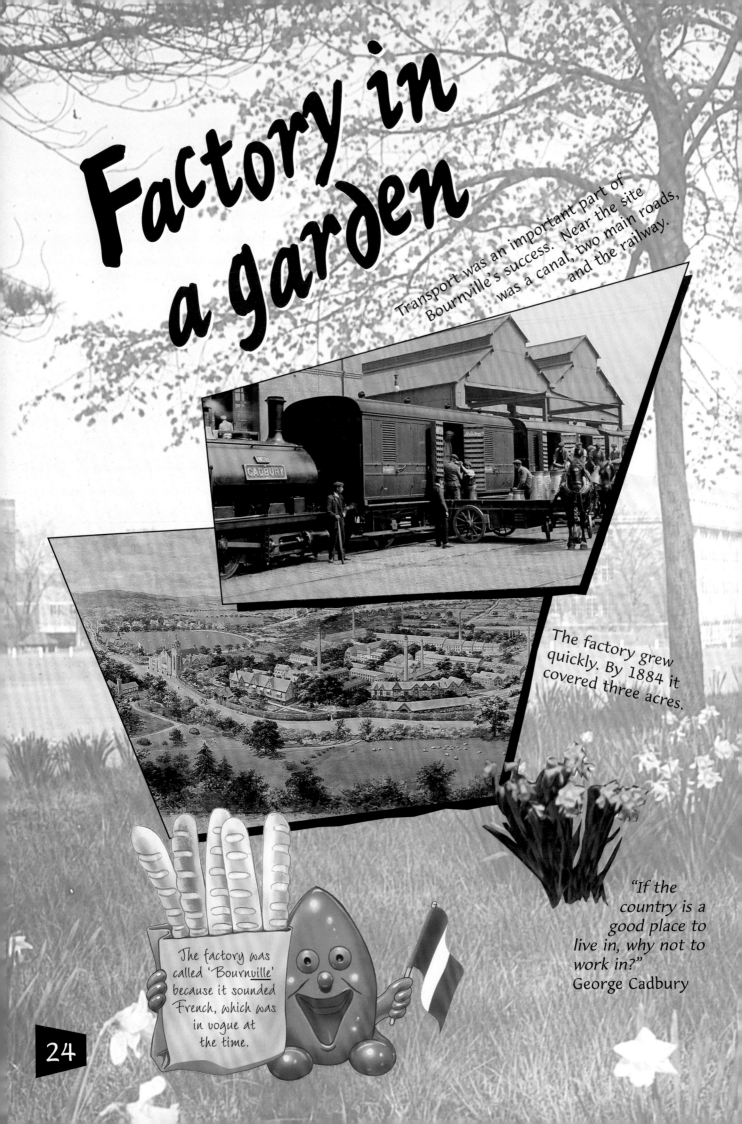

Transport was an important part of Bournville's success. Near the site was a canal, two main roads, and the railway.

The factory grew quickly. By 1884 it covered three acres.

"If the country is a good place to live in, why not to work in?"
George Cadbury

The factory was called 'Bournville' because it sounded French, which was in vogue at the time.

The Move to Bournville

By 1878, George and Richard and their 200 employees had outgrown the Bridge Street premises. In 1879 they built a new factory in $14\frac{1}{2}$ acres of meadowland near Selly Oak, on the banks of the Bourn Brook. It had the facilities they needed - including a good water supply - and room for growth.

Transports of Delight

Cocoa beans arrived from Bristol in Cadbury's own barges, on the nearby Worcester and Birmingham Canal. The company soon built its own railway sidings so that trains could bring milk in and take the finished products out.

Bigger and Better

Within ten years the number of workers had risen to 1,200. By 1919 it was 7,500! The rebuilt factory of the 1920s, much of which you can still see today, used gravity to move materials from one process to the next. Coupled with new machinery, this dramatically increased efficiency.

In the 1920s, the factory was radically altered, with steel-framed multi-storey buildings and long layouts of new machinery.

Until the 1960s, almost everything the factory used - like card boxes - was made on site.

The new factory was built on a 'greenfield' site four miles from the centre of Birmingham.

25

Healthy workers – Happy workers

George Cadbury applied his personal philosophy to his responsibilities as an employer.

Until the 1950s, men and women were strictly segregated, with their own entrances, pathways, dining rooms and working areas.

A male worker had to wear an armband to show he had permission to work in a women's area.

Elected Work Councils existe until 196

Enlightened Employers

Employees had a say in working conditions, health, safety, education and welfare policies.

When a woman married, she usually had to leave the company. She was given a bible, a carnation and a talk from a director.

Cadbury workers enjoyed progressive work practices and industrial relations. A piece-work system related payment to output, and there was a bonus for punctuality. Cadbury was the first firm to work only a half day on Saturdays, and one of the first to close the factory on Bank Holidays.

Morning prayers and bible readings enhanced the family atmosphere.

In 1906 the company provided a cash gift to start a pension fund. Trade Unions were encouraged but had limited appeal because of the excellent working conditions.

Cadbury became famous for its enlightened attitude to its workers. Many other companies followed its example.

Women's Work

Until the 1940s, most companies expected women to leave on marriage. But the labour shortage of the Second World War provided opportunities for married women to work at Cadbury.

Cadbury WORLD

Healthy workers – Happy workers

The factory offered far better medical and dental facilities than the State did – including ultraviolet treatment.

Young workers could study at the Day Continuation School. The building is now used by the University of Central England.

Employees were encouraged to learn to swim during work time.

George and Richard Cadbury didn't just build schools – they taught in them too.

As the business prospered, the company built recreation grounds, gardens and well-equipped gyms.

Friendly rivalry was developed by inter-office races.

The Girls' Swimming Baths were built in 1905.

Health and Welfare

George and Richard Cadbury wanted their staff to enjoy a healthy and active lifestyle.

The company organised outings to the country and summer camps for the young boys. Until the numbers grew too large, there was an annual party for all staff.

Many of the sports and medical facilities they provided are still used by Cadbury employees today.

A Little Learning

The Cadbury brothers were firmly committed to adult education.

Most workers joined the company straight from school aged 14. The Day Continuation School, built in 1913, allowed them to follow a broad curriculum up to the age of 16. They could study during working hours.

Other employees were allowed time off to attend evening classes.

Cadbury WORLD

Land in Trust

Cottages were built in small groups. Workers supplemented their wages by growing fruit and vegetables in the generous gardens.

The Estate was open to all, not just Cadbury workers.

Bournville inspired famous Garden Villages like Port Sunlight and Hampstead Garden Suburb.

George Cadbury established Bournville Village School in 1905.

The carillon in the school tower has 48 bells, each up to 3 tons in weight. It was inspired by one in Bruges, Belgium.

Friends Meeting House. In line with Quaker principles, there are no pubs in the 1000 acres covered by the Bournville Village Trust.

The Rest House on Bournville Green (1914) was a Silver Wedding gift to George and Elizabeth Cadbury from their employees worldwide.

Bournville – A Garden Village

George Cadbury was appalled by the slums that were the norm for most Birmingham workers. He wanted to prove that they could live in decent, affordable conditions. And, as land prices increased because of the growth of the business, he didn't want his factory in a garden hemmed in by dreary terraces erected by uncaring developers.

Model Housing

In 1893, he began Bournville village with 143 airy, cottage-style homes. As the estate grew, his vision proved to be justified. By 1915, rates of general death and infant mortality were half that for Birmingham as a whole.

In 1900, George formed the Bournville Village Trust to care for and develop his creation. Still at the forefront of housing practice, its pioneering work nowadays includes solar energy heating, energy conservation and special needs housing.

Cadbury WORLD

Family Favourites

1996 Cadbury's **Fuse**

1995 Cadbury's **Wispa Gold**

1976 Cadbury's **Caramel** *Take it easy...*

Many Cadbury products have been best sellers for decades.

1905 CADBURY'S DAIRY MILK CHOCOLATE

1908 Bournville

1915 Cadbury's *Milk Tray* ASSORTED MILK CHOCOLATES

1923 Cadbury's **creme eggs**

Cadbury William Cadbury

The famous Cadbury logo, developed from William A Cadbury's signature, was introduced in 1921.

An echo of the stylised cocoa tree is still to be found in the Cadbury World logo.

1907 CADBURY'S DAIRY MILK CHOCOLATE

1923 CADBURY'S DAIRY MILK CHOCOLATE HALF POUND NET

1933 CADBURY'S DAIRY MILK CHOCOLATE 2D

1940 CADBURY'S MILK CADBURY'S DAIRY MILK CHOCOLATE

1951 Cadbury's DAIRY MILK CHOCOLATE 8 oz

The Roses box was based on the shape of a popular 1930s ladies' handbag.

Packaging designs have changed over the years to keep Cadbury's Dairy Milk up to date.

Packaging and Design

Packaging needs to do more than just contain the product.

It has to keep it in the best possible condition. It has to display the product effectively in the shop. It has to sell - attracting and encouraging the customer to buy - and it has to be easy to use.

Our designers also have to incorporate legal requirements like description, weight and ingredients, and voluntary and commercial factors like bar codes and nutritional labelling.

The Key Ingredients

As well as the Cadbury script logo, modern designs of Cadbury's Dairy Milk feature two other essential elements. The Cadbury colours - regal purple and gold - were introduced at the beginning of the century. The 'glass and a half' was first used in advertising in 1928.

All Cadbury products include one or more of these design features.

There are over 50 packaging elements in a 454g box of Roses.

Cadbury WORLD

The first consistent Cadbury identity was the tree symbol, registered in 1911.

Family Favourites

The glass and a half has been a consistent advertising message for nearly 70 years.

CADBURY'S MILK CHOCOLATE

Advertising was important to Cadbury from the very early days.

CADBURY

A Perfect Beverage for the Young

ABSOLUTELY PURE THEREFORE BEST.

CADBURY'S DAIRY MILK CHOCOLATE

1½ GLASSES OF FULL CREAM MILK IN EVERY ½lb BLOCK

COCOA

Although spectacular, the message is simple - Milk Tray is for giving.

The famous 'man in black' commercials helped keep Milk Tray a best seller.

Memorable Advertising

Cadbury employs the most talented agencies to ensure that its advertising is as memorable as its products.

As a result, many Cadbury advertising slogans have passed into folklore. People still remember comedian Norman Vaughan and his "Roses grow on you - ooh!" from the early sixties

More modern slogans include "Thank Crunchie it's Friday" and the famous Cadbury Creme Egg question - "How do you eat yours?"

Musical Memories

But a slogan becomes most memorable when it's linked to catchy music. Often it's composed especially for the ad, such as the charming children's song used for "A finger of Fudge is just enough to give your kids a treat."

But we've also borrowed existing compositions, from Tchaikovsky ("Everyone's a Fruit and Nut case") to popular tunes such as The Banana Boat Song ("Nuts, Whole Hazelnuts - Unh!").

Every advertisement reflects the period it was made in. This one comes from the 1960s.

When London belongs to you...

Make the day with Cadburys Milk Tray

Make the day with a box of the most popular chocolates in the world – Cadburys Milk Tray. As well as your old favourites there are new ones – Lime Cordial, Hazelnut in Caramel, ... come in the

In recent years, Flake has been presented as a sensuous product for self indulgence.

Many famous stars featured in Cadbury advertising including Frank Muir, Terry Scott and Cilla Black

Cadbury WORLD

35

Gone–but not forgotten

Important Royal occasions - like a coronation - brought orders for tens of thousands of commemorative tins.

Cadbury's **Milk Tray** milk chocolate with 8 assorted centres 53 g 1.9 oz

Cadbury's **amazin'** raisin bar

Cadbury's **Aztec**

"Vogue" was in vogue from 1935 to 1959.

Although no longer available, people still remember these distinctive products.

FRUIT & NUT 8 OZ MILK CHOCOLATE 2'6

In the 1960s, people were invited to award someone the Order of the C.D.M. (Cadbury's Dairy Milk)!

ANOTHER ADVENTURE OF ELSIE AND THE BUNNY

THE Cococub NEWS

Chocolate Nostalgia

As chocolate is one of life's luxuries, it's not surprising that many of the brands have a special place in our memories. The box we received on a special occasion; the bar that comforted us on a cold wet day; and of course, the treats of childhood.

Chocolate for Children

In 1934, Cadbury introduced special tins of cocoa aimed at children, each with a free miniature animal. Nutty Squirrel, Dan Crow and Monty Monkey were eagerly collected by youngsters.

Like Elsie in the 1920s storybooks, Jonathan of the Cococub Club was always being magically whisked away to see how chocolate was made.

The club was revived after the war, as the C-Cubs led by 'Colin'. Members enjoyed a newsletter with games, quizzes and competitions.

The C-Cubs ended in 1953, to be replaced by a continuing series of special promotions for children.

Cadbury WORLD

A World of Pleasure

Cadbury Schweppes

Schweppes and its sister brands refresh people in over 100 countries

Cadbury's and Fry's chocolate products are complemented by Trebor Bassett's famous sweets.

Cadbury is an important part of a worldwide group of companies.

If you tried to eat Cadbury's annual output at one bar every five minutes, it would take you 16,000 years!

Cadbury Today

We're heavily committed to supporting education through placements, partnerships with schools and colleges, and through our "Cadbury Time" out-of-school clubs.

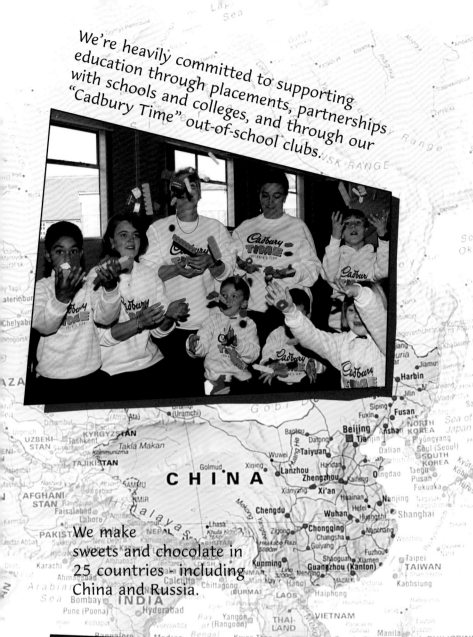

We make sweets and chocolate in 25 countries – including China and Russia.

In 1996, Cadbury began the UK's biggest ever television sponsorship, supporting Coronation Street.

Cadbury Limited is part of Cadbury Schweppes - a global business reaching over 200 countries and employing over 42,000 people.

Famous British names like Craven, Keiller, Butterkist, Barratt, Maynards and Pascall all come under the Cadbury Schweppes umbrella.

And unfamiliar Cadbury products you might encounter around the world include Googly, Perk (India), and Holey Moleys (South Africa).

A Good Neighbour

Cadbury Schweppes contributes actively to local communities. Amongst many examples, we have:

- *supported* the Nelson Mandela Children's Fund;
- *assisted* Operation Raleigh and expeditions to Everest and the Antarctic;
- *aided* medical research into multiple sclerosis, diabetes and cancer;
- *sponsored* sports including basketball in South Africa and table tennis in Nigeria.

Cadbury WORLD

The Chocolate Experience

Because of hygiene regulations, a Moulded Packaging Plant is the only part of the factory open to visitors.

Chocolates made traditionally by hand in the Demonstration Area.

Have you enjoyed Chuckle Bean' chocolate facts throughout this brochure?

Cadbury World was officially opened by Prime Minister John Major on 12 April 1991.

Fun in the Fantasy Factory - for kids, or anyone who likes pushing buttons.

A chance to work off all that free chocolate!

Cadbury World

By 1970, millions of people had enjoyed a factory tour of Bournville, but the tours had to end because of health and hygiene considerations. Cadbury World opened in 1990, in response to many thousands of requests from people who still wanted an insight into the first name in chocolate.

A fascinating multi-media experience tells the history of chocolate, from the ancient Mayas right up to the present day. There's a chance to taste the *chocolatl* of the Aztecs, clock in as a Bournville worker, and search for Cadbury magic on the *Cadabra* ride.

Much of the exhibition relates to National Curriculum subjects including history, geography and science. Many schools find that a visit to Cadbury World is a fun way to bring these subjects alive.

The Sweet Smell of Success

Cadbury World is now one of Britain's leading attractions, with over half a million visitors every year.

The biggest addition to Cadbury World is a magical ride - Cadabra.